FIVE 5 FINGER PIANO

MODERN MOVIE
FAVORITES

ISBN 978-1-5400-0051-4

HAL•LEONARD®

7777 W. BLUEMOUND RD. P.O. BOX 13819 MILWAUKEE, WI 53213

Visit Hal Leonard Online at
www.halleonard.com

4   **CAN'T STOP THE FEELING**........... Trolls

16   **CITY OF STARS**.................................. La La Land

11   **EVERMORE**.......................................Beauty and the Beast

26   **EVERYTHING IS AWESOME (AWESOME REMIX!!!)**...................... The Lego Movie

28   **HOW FAR I'LL GO** .... Moana

38   **SPIRIT IN THE SKY** .... Guardians of the Galaxy

21   **TRY EVERYTHING** .... Zootopia

34   **UNFORGETTABLE** .... Finding Dory

Can't Stop the Feeling
from TROLLS

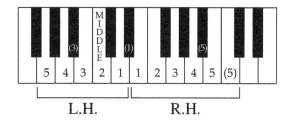

Words and Music by Justin Timberlake, Max Martin and Shellback

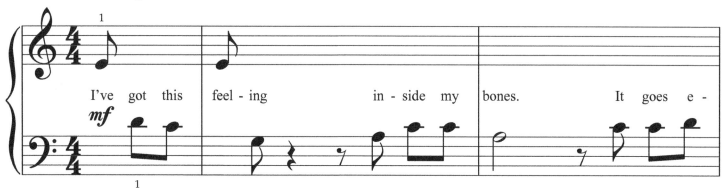

Duet Part (Student plays one octave higher than written.)

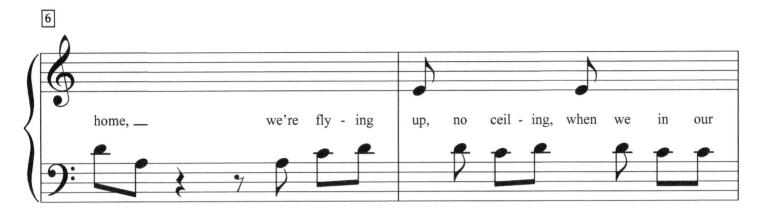

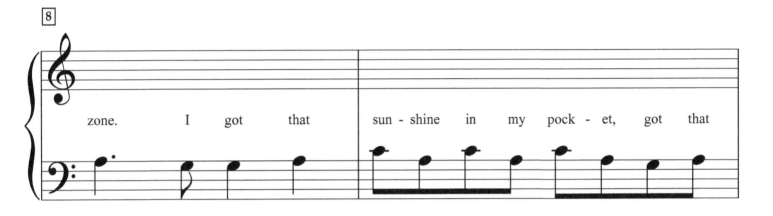

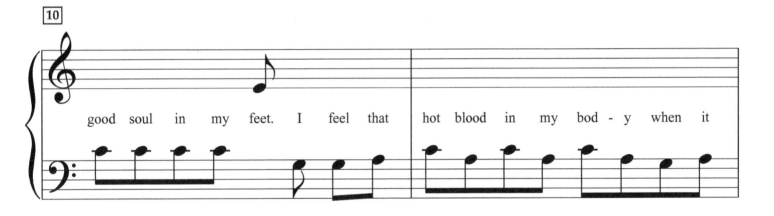

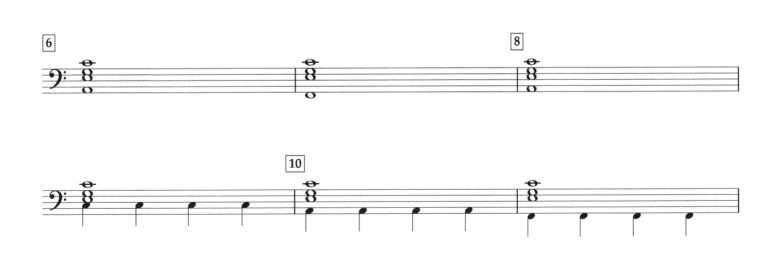

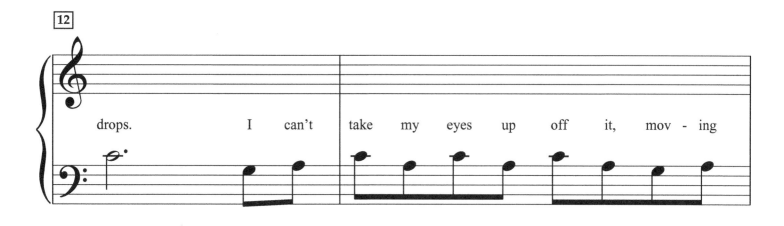

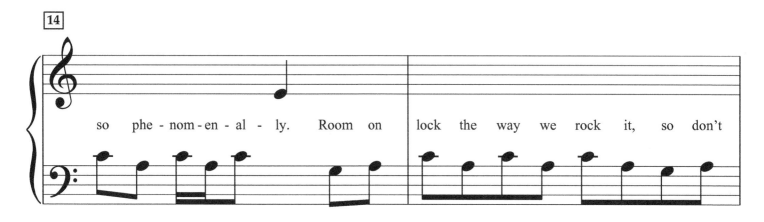

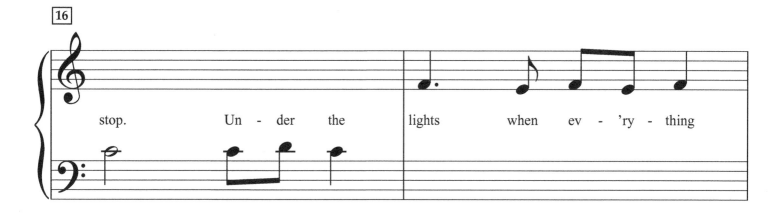

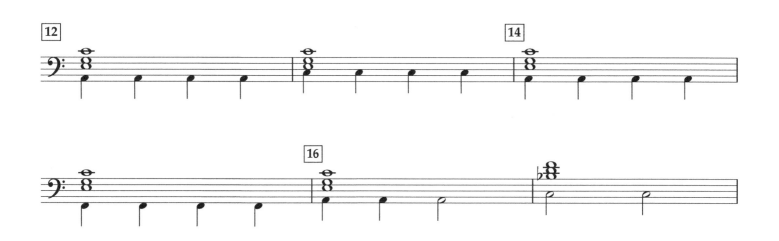

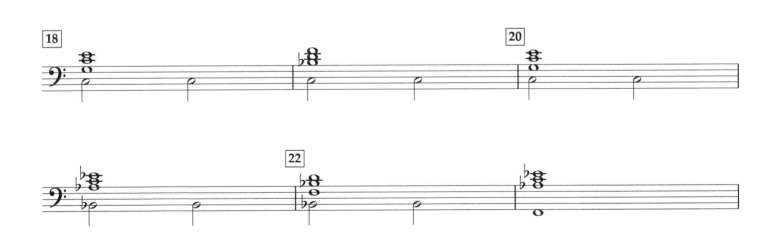

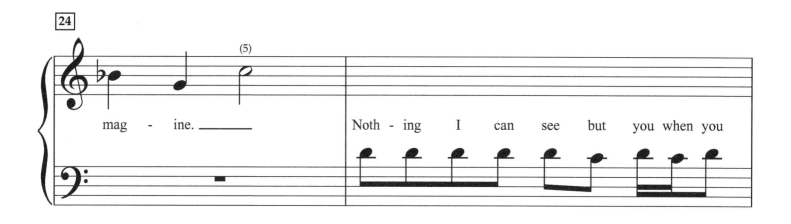

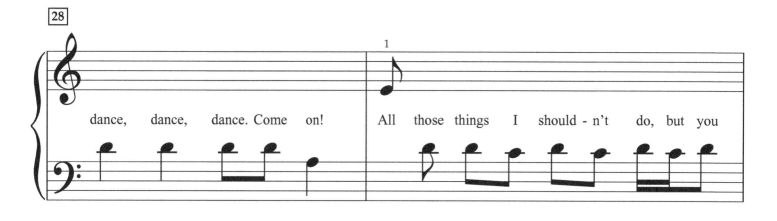

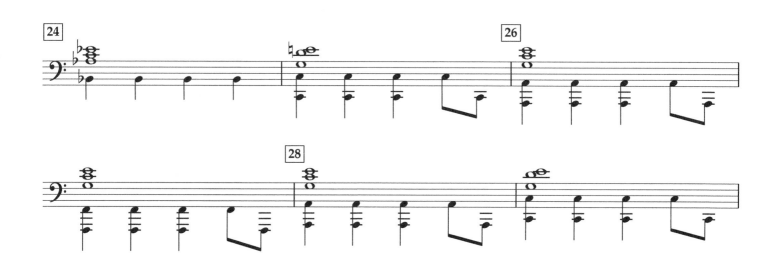

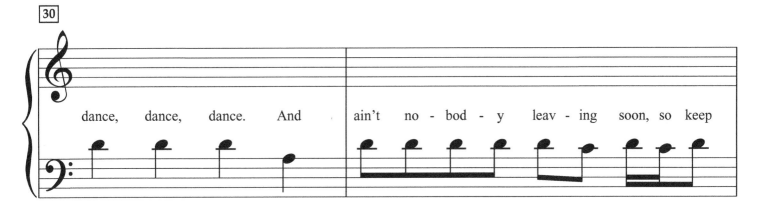

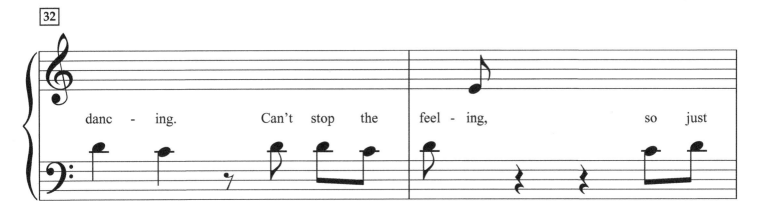

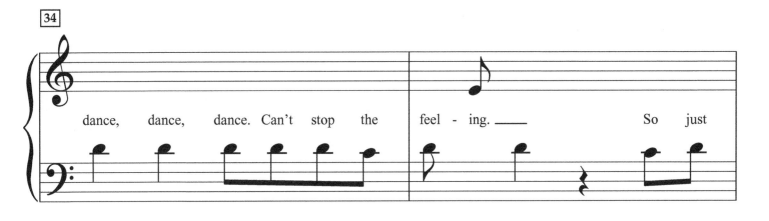

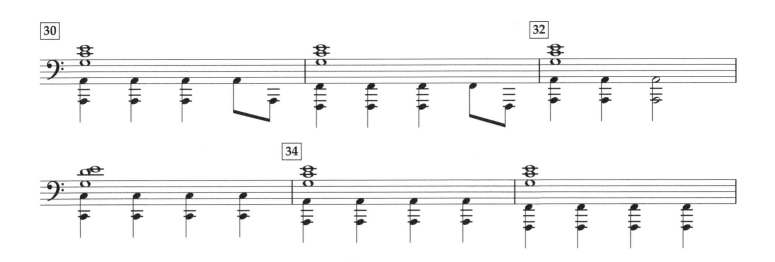

9

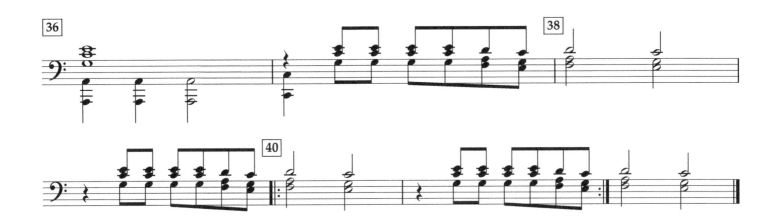

Evermore
from BEAUTY AND THE BEAST

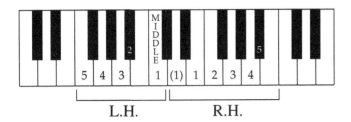

Music by Alan Menken
Lyrics by Tim Rice

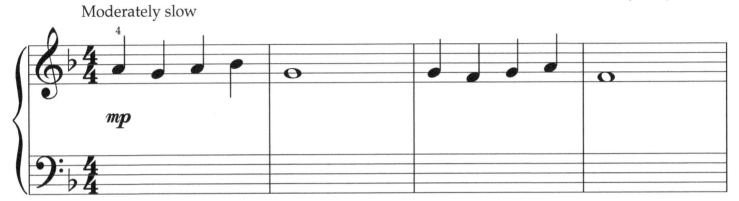

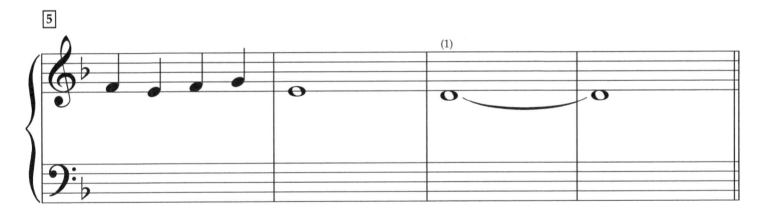

Duet Part (Student plays one octave higher than written.)

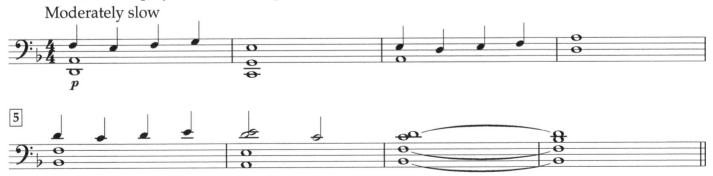

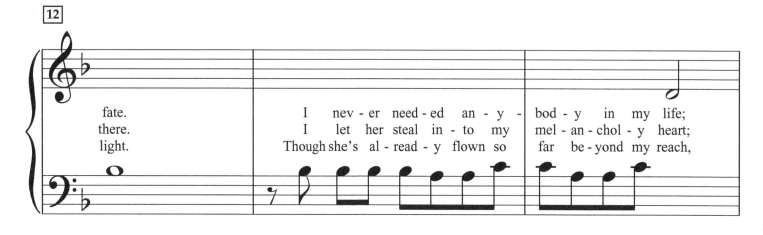

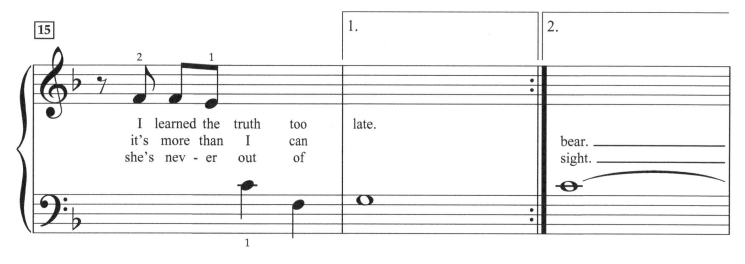

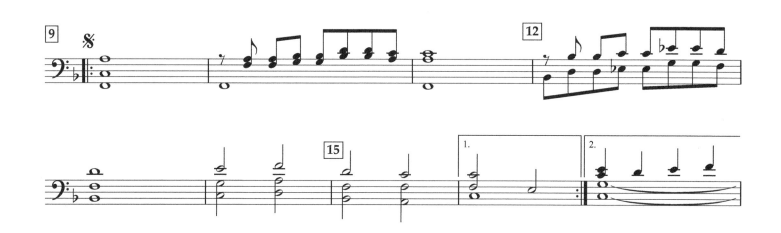

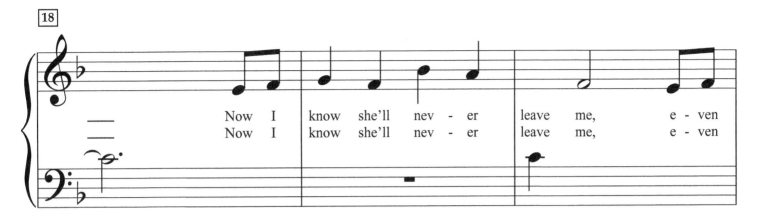

Now I know she'll nev - er leave me, e - ven
Now I know she'll nev - er leave me, e - ven

as she runs a - way. She will still tor - ment me,
as she fades from view. She will still in - spire me,

calm me, hurt me, move me, come what may. }
be a part of ev - 'ry - thing I do. }

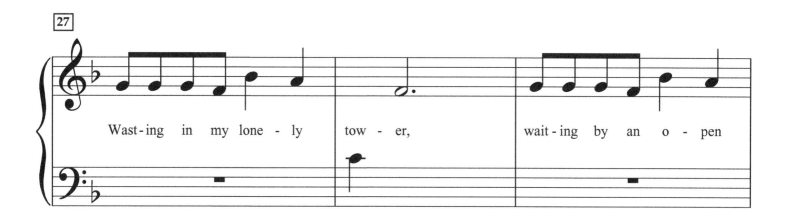

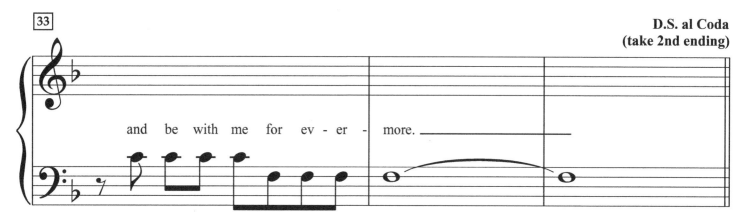

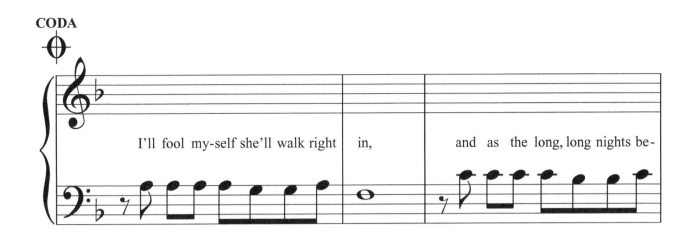

CODA

I'll fool my-self she'll walk right in, and as the long, long nights be-

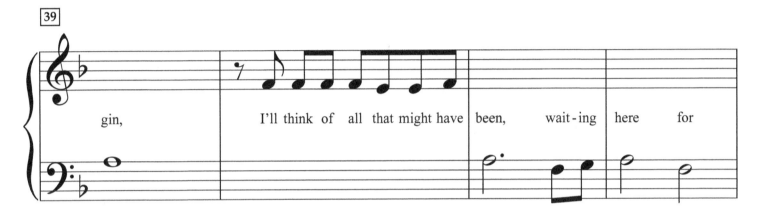

39

gin, I'll think of all that might have been, wait-ing here for

43

ev - er - more.

(1)

CODA

39

43

City of Stars
from LA LA LAND

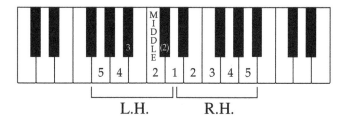

Music by Justin Hurwitz
Lyrics by Benj Pasek & Justin Paul

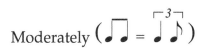

Cit-y of stars, ___ are you shin-ing just for me? ___

Cit-y of stars, ___ there's so much that I can't see. ___ Who

Duet Part (Student plays one octave higher than written.)

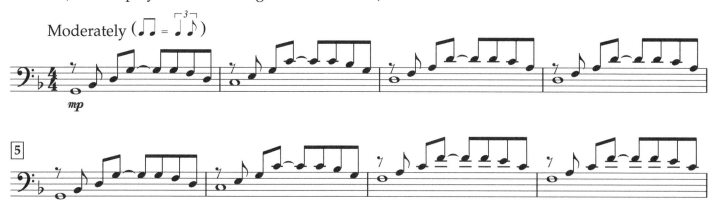

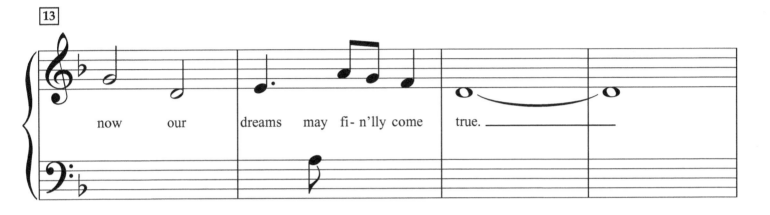

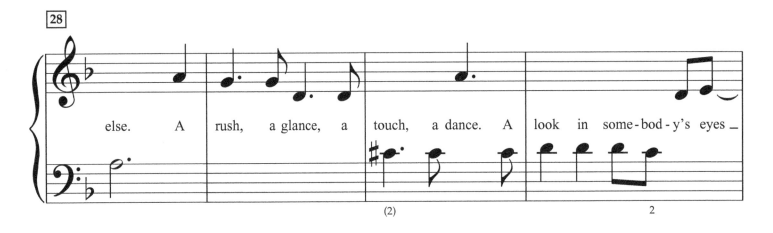

this cra-zy feel-ing, a _rat-tat-tat on my heart..._ _Think I want it to_ _stay._

(2)

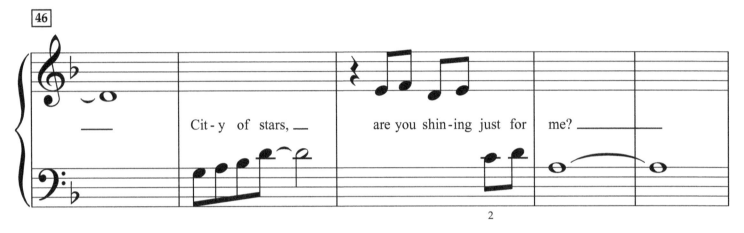

Cit-y of stars, _are you shin-ing just for_ _me?_

2

Cit-y of stars, _you nev-er shined so_ _bright-ly._

(2)

42   46

51

Try Everything
from ZOOTOPIA

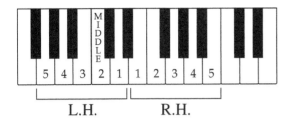

Words and Music by Sia Furler,
Tor Erik Hermansen and Mikkel Eriksen

Dance beat

Duet Part (Student plays one octave higher than written.)
Dance beat

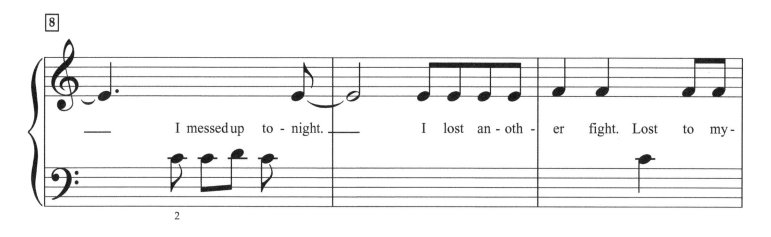

I messed up to - night. I lost an - oth - er fight. Lost to my-

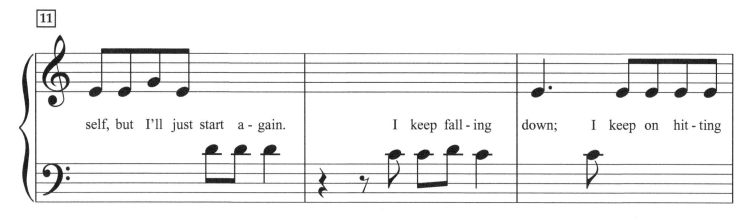

self, but I'll just start a - gain. I keep fall - ing down; I keep on hit - ting

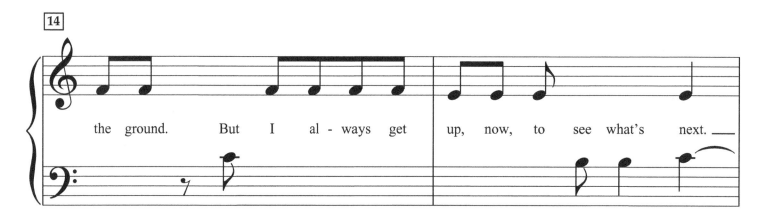

the ground. But I al - ways get up, now, to see what's next.

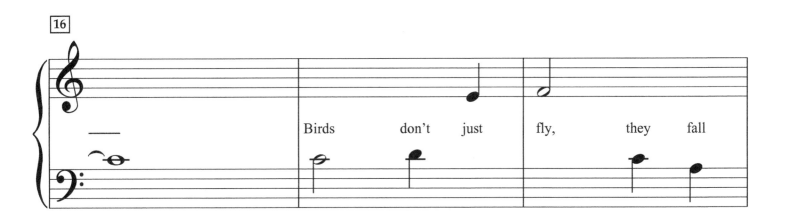

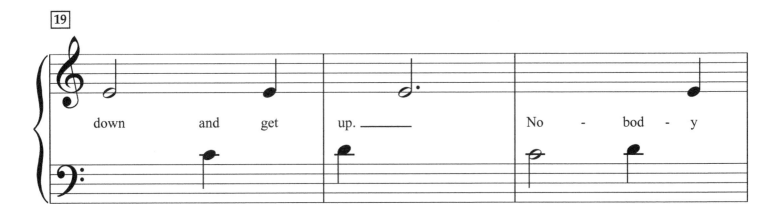

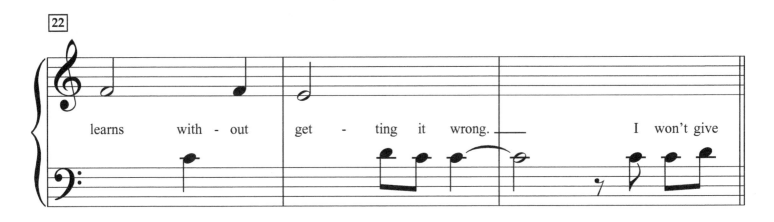

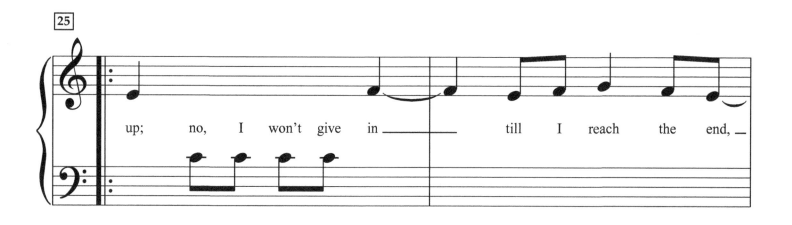

up; no, I won't give in ____ till I reach the end, __

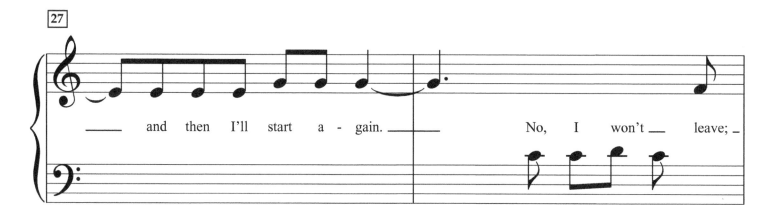

____ and then I'll start a - gain. ____ No, I won't __ leave; __

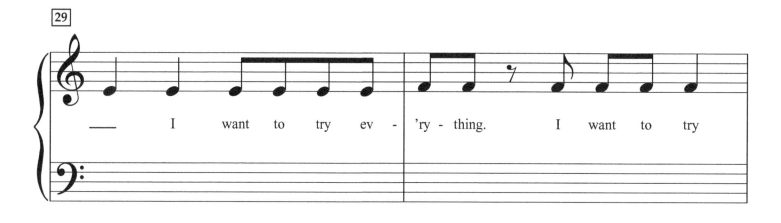

__ I want to try ev - 'ry - thing. I want to try

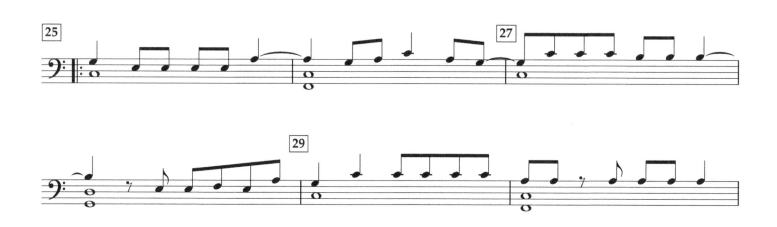

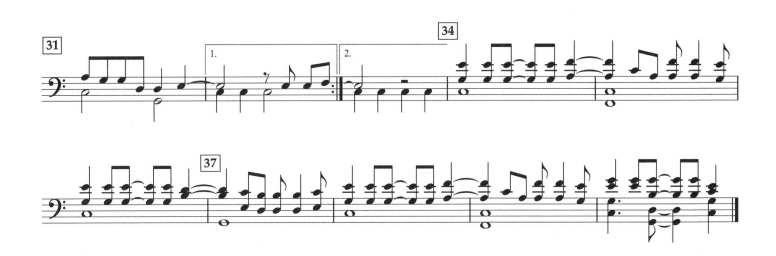

Everything Is Awesome
(Awesome Remix!!!)
from THE LEGO MOVIE

Words by Shawn Patterson
Music by Andrew Samberg,
Jorma Taccone, Akiva Schaffer,
Joshua Bartholomew, Lisa Harriton
and Shawn Patterson

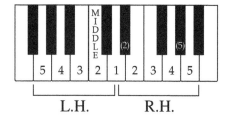

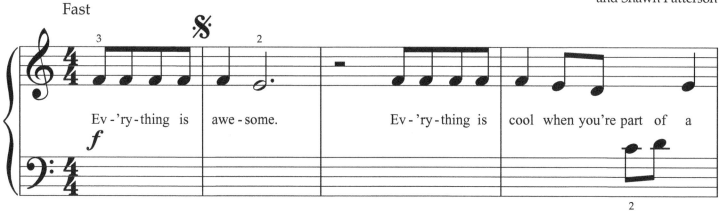

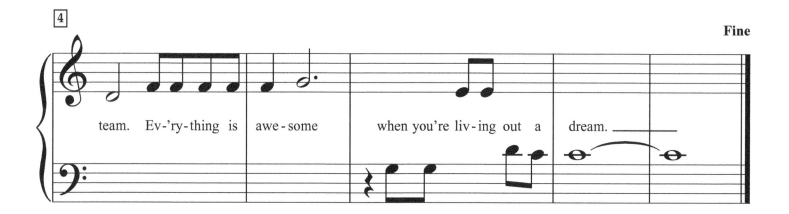

Duet Part (Student plays one octave higher than written.)

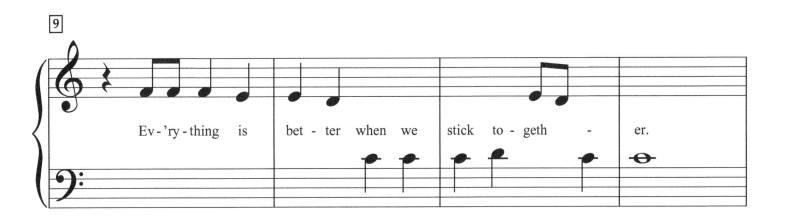

How Far I'll Go
from MOANA

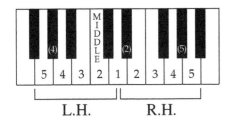

Music and Lyrics by
Lin-Manuel Miranda

Moderately

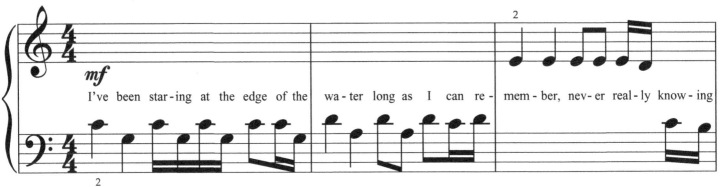

I've been star-ing at the edge of the wa-ter long as I can re- mem-ber, nev-er real-ly know-ing

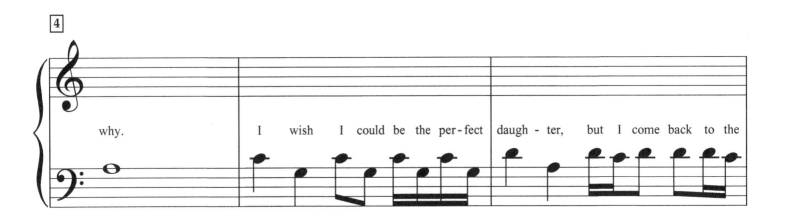

why. I wish I could be the per-fect daugh-ter, but I come back to the

Duet Part (Student plays one octave higher than written.)

Moderately

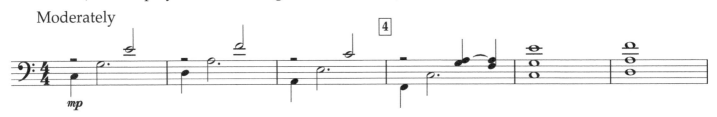

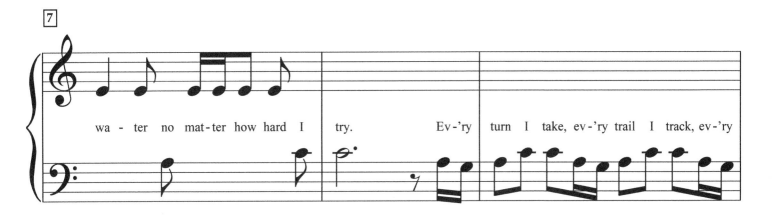

wa - ter no mat-ter how hard I try. Ev-'ry turn I take, ev-'ry trail I track, ev-'ry

path I make, ev-'ry road leads back to the place I know where I can-not go, where I long to be. See the

(4)

line where the sky meets the sea, it calls ____ me, and no one knows ____ how far it

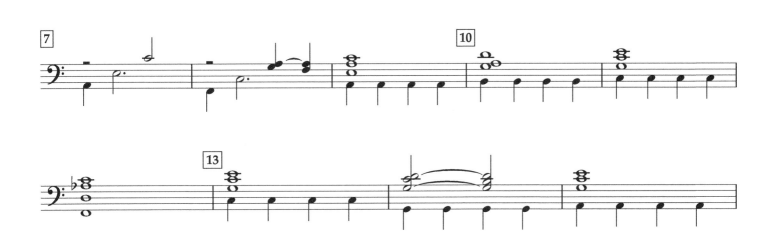

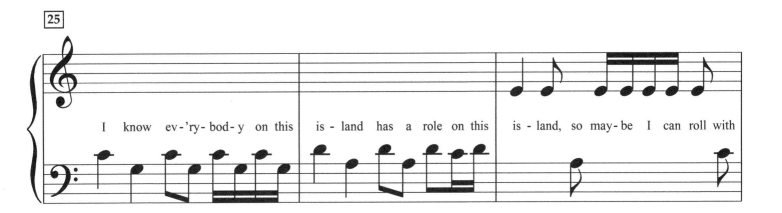

light as it shines on the sea: it's blind - ing, but no one knows _____ how deep it

goes. _____ And it seems like it's call - ing out to me, so come find _____

_____ me and let me know. _____ What's be - yond that line? Will I cross that line? The

Unforgettable
featured in FINDING DORY

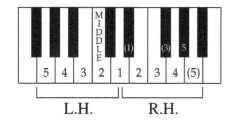

Words and Music by
Irving Gordon

Duet Part (Student plays one octave higher than written.)

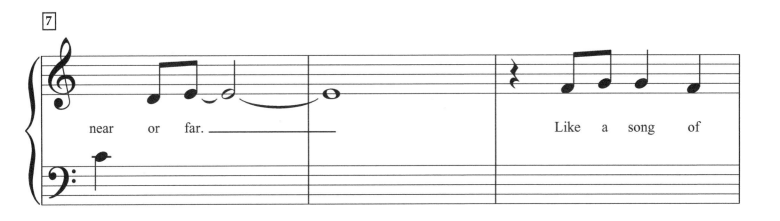

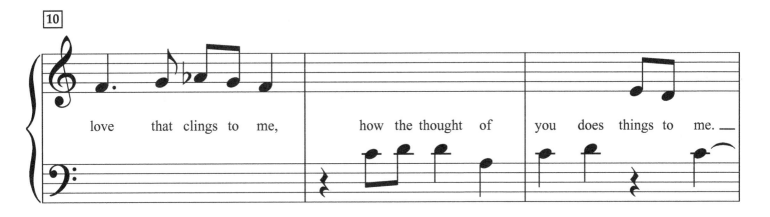

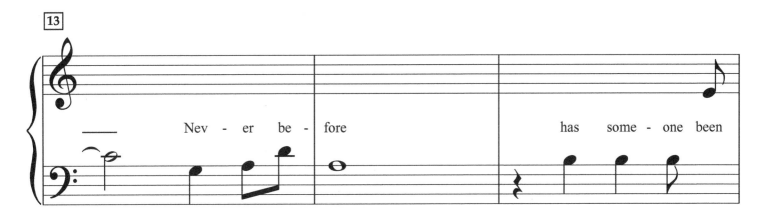

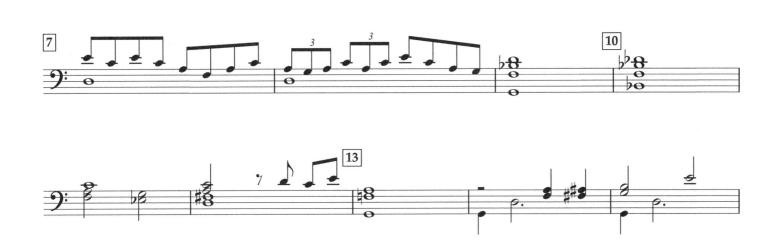

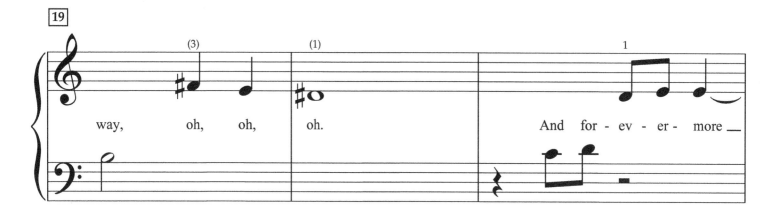

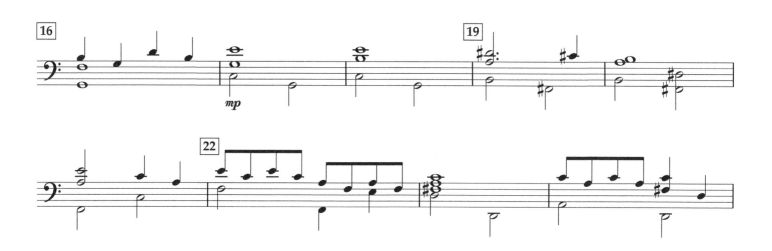

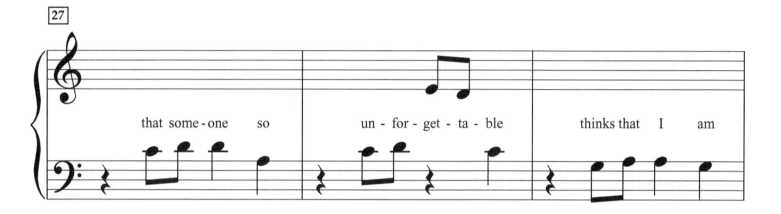

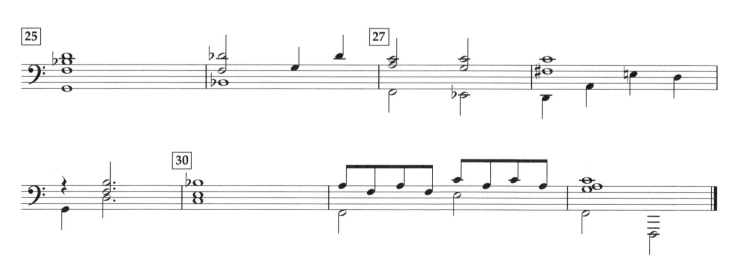

Spirit in the Sky
featured in GUARDIANS OF THE GALAXY

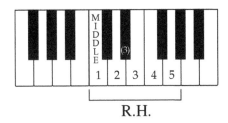

Words and Music by
Norman Greenbaum

Moderately

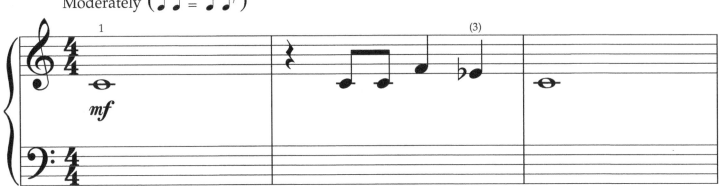

When I die and they lay me to rest, ___

Duet Part (Student plays one octave higher than written.)

Moderately

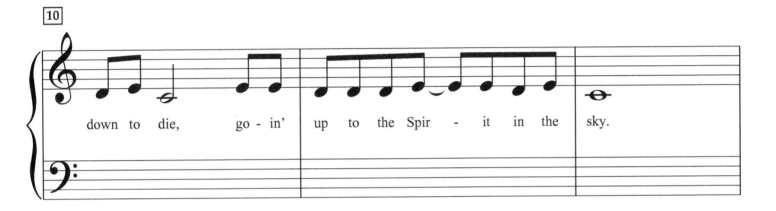